Praise f

MW00623100

"Erica Goss's collection of poems and inspirational exercises, *Vibrant Words: Ideas and Inspirations for Poets*, teaches poets to peel back the noise to find the kernels of poetic story that will appeal universally." —**Serena M. Agusto-Cox**, poet and reviewer at *Savvy Verse & Wit* and *War Through the Generations*

"Erica Goss presents inspiring tips, techniques, strategies, observations, and insights accrued through study and direct experience. Her book will prove a useful guide for new and experienced writers alike, especially those struggling to navigate a 'dry spell,' desiring a poetic nudge, or seeking authentic creative direction." —**John Amen**, editor of *The Pedestal Magazine*

"With her friendly, non-intimidating approach, Erica Goss coaxes out the poet in all of us. Open this treasure chest anywhere and do what the page says to do. Although these prompts were written for poets, many also work well for prose writers." —**Ann Marie Brown**, travel writer, magazine editor, writing instructor at Sierra Nevada College

"Many good prompts here, nudges to get you started if you're a beginner, or shoves if you're further along, but find yourself stuck." —**Nils Peterson**, Santa Clara County Poet Laureate Emeritus

"Do not attempt to read this book without pen and paper, for inspiration leaps from every page. Original, fun prompts and ideas are illustrated with masterfully selected poems. This winning combination stirs the reader to write. Valuable creativity tips are shared in an accessible way in this practical, inspired and inspiring book! Erica Goss has produced a true gift to poets!" —**Katerina Stoykova-Klemer**, author of *The Porcupine of Mind* and *Bigger Than They Appear: Anthology of Very Short Poems*

"Erica Goss's *Vibrant Words* is a little gem of poetry prompts: concise, efficient, whimsical, immediate.... What a delight to read! Each of these prompts offers useful guidance with inspirational suggestions, ideas, and examples for poets and all poetry lovers. This is also a welcome tool for poetry workshops and other related settings." —**Fiona Sze-Lorrain**, author of *My Funeral Gondola* (2013) and *Water the Moon* (2010)

"Erica Goss's elegantly conceived and thoughtfully edited *Vibrant Words* will assist and inspire many an aspiring poet and storyteller. Like other artists, wordsmiths should welcome and respond to the challenges of surprise and demand. These warm, prodding pages quiver with enough prompts, suggestions, exercises, examples and borderline ecstasy to keep any fledgling or practiced writer of poetry meaningfully focused and sharp for a lifetime." —**Al Young**, California's Poet Laureate Emeritus

Vibrant Words:

ideas and inspirations for poets

Also By Erica Goss
Wild Place: Poems

May this book inspire your writing!

Vibrant Words:

ideas and inspirations for poets

By Erica Goss

Erica Goss

4-2-14

PUSHPEN PRESS | SAN JOSÉ CALIFORNIA

Copyright © 2014 ALL RIGHTS RESERVED by authors and
artists. No part of this book may be reproduced or transmitted
in any form by any means, electronic or mechanical, including
photocopying and recording, or by any information storage and
retrieval system, except as, may be expressly permitted in writing
from the publisher. Request for permission should be addressed to
ericagoss@comcast.net.

Library of Congress Cataloging-in-Publication Data is Available.

ISBN 978-0-9896676-3-0

Printed in the United States of America 2014
All rights reserved.

EXECUTIVE EDITOR AND ARTISTIC DIRECTOR
Steve "Spike" Wong

LAYOUT AND DESIGN
Jan McCutcheon

COVER PHOTOGRAPH
Erica Goss

*Dedicated to my parents, Edith Pferdekamp Goss
and Robert Tweedie Goss, who encouraged a love of
literature and the arts in all of their children.*

Contents

Introduction

I started writing poetry as a child. Back then, I had so many ideas that it seemed impossible to get them all on the page. All I had to do at that young age was look around me: my family, friends, and the back yard were enough to get me writing.

As I grew older, I discovered the world of poetry prompts. I was charmed and fascinated to learn that poets used various tips and tricks. I was surprised that some people looked down on these prompts, as if poems should arrive unbidden.

Some poems do arrive, almost complete, seemingly out of thin air. However, as most writers inevitably learn, waiting for inspiration is mostly just waiting. Poems can and should be actively sought, captured, and written down.

The ideas in this book are tried and true. I use them all, often. I enjoy collecting writing exercises that work for me and sharing them with friends and fellow poets. Like snowflakes, no two are exactly alike, but all are equally valuable.

I'm happy to include writing exercises from Dave Bonta, Kelly Cressio-Moeller, Pushpa MacFarlane, Jennifer Swanton Brown, Connie Post, Evelyn So, Ellaraine Lockie, and Eileen Malone. They have inspired me with their poems, and I treasure these prompts.

May this book open your writing to new possibilities.

Erica Goss
Los Gatos, CA
2014

Holidays

Nils Peterson, the first Poet Laureate of Santa Clara County, writes a poem every Christmas. He collected his poems in a chapbook titled *For This Day* from Frog on the Moon Press (2005). Is there a holiday that moves you to write? Or a particular day that inspires? List the major holidays and let their associations come to you. For some reason, I have written a number of Easter poems. Here is "Easter Sunday:"

Erica Goss

Easter Sunday

Joy comes, grief goes, we know not how
- James Russell Lowell

1.
After a rigid winter
with too many days
spent in classrooms,
the faint presence of birds
disturbs the windowsills.

Trees open their mouths,
fine-cut leaves cup air –
careful, the way a woman
slides a hand beneath
her child's oval
skull and lifts
his face to hers.

2.
I have been too loyal
to grief. I have
given corners to darkness,
allowed myself

to think love shrinks, cold.
Now when sorrow answers
it doesn't matter.
I tell my own stories,

place colored eggs
under shrubs, behind stones,
coddle a few in a flowerpot.
One by one, children
take them back,

heads tempera bulbs
in morning's convocation.
Joy scrambles sadness. Lord,
break this day over my head.
Light sticks to me like yolk.

First published in Zoland Poetry 5

Occasional Poetry

Richard Blanco wrote a poem for President Obama's second inauguration. It's not easy to write poems about occasions – i.e., "occasional poetry" – but Blanco did an exceptional job. You can write an occasional poem about any event you choose: having a meal with a friend, getting up in the morning, a graduation, wedding, or funeral. Small occasions are often the times we remember the most, so why not try your hand at memorializing one in poetry? For an example, read "O Captain My Captain" by Walt Whitman.

Erica Goss

I wrote "The Kindness of Trees" to commemorate the opening
of Pageant Park in Los Gatos in April 2013, which was also
in honor of Arbor Day. The poem is written in the form of a
pantoum.

The Kindness of Trees

Breathing us as we breathe them,
the trees are kind to us.
They take the brunt of sun and crows,
calm our cities, tame our thoughts.

The trees are kind to us.
We can never pay them back.
Calm our cities, tame our thoughts,
moderate our voices.

We can never pay them back.
Each one's a place of refuge.
Moderate our voices
as we gather in the shade.

Each one's a place of refuge,
strong yet wordless, murmuring.
We gather in the shade.

Now the clouds are coming down.

Strong yet wordless, murmuring,
they take the brunt of sun and crows.
Now the clouds are coming down,
breathing us as we breathe them.

Moments

The poet Lucien Stryk passed away on January 24, 2013. He was born in Poland in 1924. I have turned to his marvelous collection, *Of Pen and Ink and Paper Scraps* (Ohio University Press, 1989) frequently. Every poem in this book is a delight. Stryk is a master at capturing a moment and telling its story with a kind of revelatory tenderness: a brief, intense experience. His poem, "Dreaming to Music," is an example of that depth.

Try your hand at the exploration of time: slow down a fleeting glimpse, detail it, write down its odd juxtapositions.

11

Erica Goss

Stryk leaps from "As I / turn up the stereo" to "a girl in Rheims / walks out of a medieval / love song".

Jump, fearlessly, into your poem.

Ekphrasis

Ekphrasis is the response of one art form to another. Write a poem about a work of art. It can be a painting, sculpture, photograph, music, or another poem or piece of writing. A few years ago, I wrote the following poems about photographs by the famous photographer, Edward S. Curtis, who took iconic (but not always accurate) pictures of the vanishing Native American tribes:

Erica Goss

Crater Lake, 1923

I stood before the lake
one summer day

minerals fell
silent fragments

all at once
the souls of children rose up together

headed west
over the valley

surrender
not grief

nothing rippled
the lake's surface

An Oasis in the Badlands, 1905

This land has not saved us.
My horse drinks here
for the last time.
Winter will come, unaware
of how I leaned back in the saddle
as my animal filled herself,
the river emptying
under her hooves;
loss wears away
to black and white
soft like ashes after
a prairie fire.

First published in Ekphrasis, *Spring/Summer 2009*

Love

The poetry of love: consider this poem by Mary Lou Taylor:

When I First Awoke

I want
pockets full of marbles
jacks and a ball

A lustrous floor
me dancing

Erica Goss

with open arms

Spring
to return again
that trembling season

I want to relive
that moment of fire
when I first
awoke to love

From The Fringes of Hollywood, *Jacaranda Press, 2002*

About writing the poem, Mary Lou wrote, "I was taking a day class from Ken Weisner. I sat in my car scribbling and eating a brown bag lunch. That's the poem that came out, and I walked into class and read it. No edit on that poem. I wish all were that easy to write." The poem does feel fresh and immediate, filled with longing for connection and romance. How can we write a poem that leaps off the page like this one? We're not always so lucky as to receive an entire poem in one draft.

Mary Lou's poem works because of its details. Short as it is, it's a biography of emotions, moving quickly from childhood to adolescence to adulthood. Reading it brought up wave after wave of memories, from playing jacks with other children during school recess, to my first high school dance, to the sudden joy of a first crush, and the Earth's yearly renewal of Spring. Notice that the poem is not addressed to anyone in particular; rather, it focuses on love itself.

Begin by making two lists: how you feel when you are in love, and how you feel when love is over. Use specifics, and avoid clichés. Examine your lists and see where the story is.

Faithful Husband of the Rain

Water is always scarce in California, and we grow up here aware of how valuable it is. One of my sons was born in a drought year, and the other in a wet one. In "Water," Wendell Berry describes his fear of drought:

And all my life I have dreaded the return
of that year, sure that it still is
somewhere, like a dead enemy's soul.
Fear of dust in my mouth is always with me...

Erica Goss

Water is life, yet we waste it thoughtlessly until confronted by
its absence:

My sweetness is to wake in the night
after days of dry heat, hearing the rain.

Write a poem about water. Our bodies are at least 90%
water, and all of the water on Earth is 3.5 billion years old.
In Genesis, the water is already there: "and the spirit of God
moved upon the face of the waters." Were you born in a dry
year? An exceptionally wet one? If you don't know, ask your
parents. If they don't know, invent it!

I Left My Heart in the Los Angeles Basin

Have you ever been completely in love with a city? It's no wonder that people leave their hearts in San Francisco, fall in love in Paris, and endlessly adore New York, in all of its various moods and guises. In his poem "Chicago," Carl Sandburg wrote, "Come and show me another city with lifted head singing / so proud to be alive and coarse and strong and cunning." Who can forget the "Floral loops / Of the freeway" and the "calligraphy of cars" from Gary Snyder's "Night Song of the Los Angeles Basin?"

Erica Goss

Begin by listing your impressions of a city you love. Why do you love it? Are there details about the city that only you know? Make us want to be there so much that it's all we can do not to jump in the car, drive to the airport, and take the first plane there.

Here is a beautiful poem from Joie Cook, who left us February 24, 2013:

There Are Nights In San Francisco

There are nights in San Francisco
When even the bedbugs come out to pray
Amongst the forest that is life here

And streets I believe I've been on before
Become hallucinations,
Every steep hill climbed,
An applause for gravity...

But I've taken it for granted
For over 30 years
The seven hills, the cable cars,
The view from Twin Peaks
On a crisp, November night...

I Left My Heart in the Los Angeles Basin

I fall in love with cities
The way most people fall in love,
Shamelessly hopeful in the beginning,
Careless, naïve and blind…

And there are nights in San Francisco
I would wish to forget
Like a waning romance,
Waiting to crash,
Never looking back
At the wreckage behind.

Delusions of an Erasure Poet: The Shadow Text

By Dave Bonta

There is — I've come to feel — a text within the text, made up of the words and phrases that lodge most firmly in our minds as we read and the hidden relationships we sense between them. Can it be brought into the light and given at least a minimal coherence? If so, what if anything might it tell us about the parent text?

I think this shadow text is based in part on semi-conscious, momentary misinterpretations which we are continually correcting automatically as we read. It's of a piece with those false ideas and associations we all harbor based on misunderstandings that were subsequently corrected, sometimes very quickly, but still too late to prevent such shadow ideas from persisting, showing up in dreams and sometimes even influencing conscious thoughts. (This is, in part, how propaganda works.)

If I were able to read with perfect focus, perhaps a shadow text would not develop, but the imagination is an unruly beast, and fluent reading gives it latitude to stray to one side or another as I proceed, like a dog on a long leash inspecting things of interest while its owner plods straight ahead. It has, in other words, its own agenda. To recover the text within a text, do we not also need to be dog-like and follow our ears and noses more than our eyes? Certainly we need to be more active. Investigation may even require that we bark and listen for a response.

Delusions of an Erasure Poet: The Shadow Text

Here is an erasure poem from the diary of Samuel Pepys:

After talking about going to sea,
after drinking with a butcher and a violin,
after bacon, capons and fritters,
after singing and drinking,
after a dance or two with my lord,
soberly and without fear
I lay awake.

Very Short Poems

Katerina Stoykova-Klemer edited *Bigger Than They Appear: Anthology of Very Short Poems* (Accents Publishing, Kentucky, 2011). The criteria for each poem's length is that it be no longer than 50 words, including the title. Here are a few examples:

Silhouette

By Peggy Landsman

If you weren't you and I weren't I
We two could live as one

But I *am* I
You are stuck

Standing in old friends' doorways
Wearing unflattering shoes.

fable

By Mark DeCarteret

I've had
no luck
finding
the forest
I was supposed
to have been
lost in
forever
and ever

Nose

By Paul Hostovsky

Hers the only
red leaf in winter
that never fell

Yes, these are addicting. I just can't stop reading them.
To get a short poem just right takes skill and patience.
Perhaps you have several short poems hiding in a longer
poem. Short poems exist in newspaper headlines, in ad-
vertisements, on T-shirts. Spend the day looking for the
magic in short phrases. Then write them down, but don't
take too long!

Short on Time? Try a Zip Poem

By Jennifer Swanton Brown

If you're committed to writing poems regularly, sometimes all you've got is short time – and if you want to exercise your brain and poetry muscles, you need a short poem form to help you out. A snatch of found language, a snippet of an image, a catchy overheard meter – anything small can be all you need to get started.

Michael Dylan Welch, the first Poet Laureate of Redmond, Washington, is a renowned poet, specializing in Japanese traditional forms. You can check out his work starting with his blog Graceguts. Michael shared the news in December

35

2013 that the English poet, John Carley, had passed away after a four-year battle with cancer. Michael challenged us, as a way to celebrate Carley's life, to write a poem in the zip haiku format he invented. Never having heard of a zip haiku, I was intrigued! Turns out the zip is a delightful little (and surprisingly powerful) form.

According to a 2001 article by Carley, a zip is "proposed as an analogue to the Japanese haiku, but uses a form more suited to the innate phonic and semantic qualities of English. The zip employs fifteen syllables, two weak pauses and one strong. The poem is centred on the caesura."

What could be better? A short form for the crazy holiday season, or those dark days when I am stuck at work late, exhausted, grumpy, etc. And a "real" form, one created, as so many forms are, when one ancient vital language tradition moves as a living thing will to another culture. Think sonnets traipsing across Europe from Italy to England. Think Pantoum sailing out from Malaysia and now sprinkled across the US. So, with centuries of poetic momentum behind me, I took up the challenge of writing a zip.

The first is a moment remembered from my daughter's beach party and the second is a reflection on my mother's upcoming birthday in Maine.

#1

making faces   around the fire

beer bottles   marshmallow smoke

#2

January   glittering blue and white

the shape of   windows

You can find more examples in the Carley article cited above. You can read more about the theory behind zips in the Archives of the World Haiku Review.

To write your own, start by jotting down several images that cluster around an observation or a memory. Focus on verbs and nouns, avoid metaphor if possible. Think about seasons. Then just play with the syllable count and the line breaks. I wrote at least 25 versions of the #2 zip above before I was happy with the balance and the mood. Don't be fooled – a short poem can be just as challenging, but it doesn't take so long because there are fewer words to shuffle about.

Have fun!

Journal Lines

What do these lines have in common?

within the long story of you and me
surfaces of my life
storms predicted for tonight
I was chased & lost the race
listen to poems in Polish
everything waits for me on paper
smeary edges like an old tattoo
there's no love on the moon

Erica Goss

dead/glossy/feathers
already white mold
a fern's narrative
skin craves a new climate

These are all lines from my current journal that found their way into poems. Today's prompt is simple: if you don't already keep a journal, begin now! Write down the random things people say. Write down why the sky reminds you of your father's laugh. Write lines from poetry that strike you. Do this every day. Do it several times per day. When people ask you where you get your ideas, smile and say nothing. Then open your journal, and start writing.

Variations on a Theme

The composer, Sir Edward Elgar, wrote "Variations on an Original Theme for Orchestra ('Enigma')", using a simple tune of only four notes. This piece has thirteen movements. I wondered if I could use a similar premise: four words, images, or patterns, to write a poem in thirteen stanzas. Let's give it try. Select words or images that have multiple possibilities: nouns that become verbs (i.e., "watch" and "play") and words that have homonyms, such as "see" and "sea." Take it as far as you can, and have fun!

Prove This Wrong

Marvin Bell's poem "To Dorothy" starts "You are not beautiful, exactly." Bell quickly rescues the mood – and his marriage – with the next line, "You are beautiful, inexactly." The negative can be a lot of fun, and useful when stuck revising a poem that seems dead on the page. Try the following and see if you can revitalize a lackluster poem, or kick loose some new ideas:

It wasn't a sunny day
He didn't seem too bright
The food didn't impress me
The landscape wasn't at all like the travel brochure's picture
The gift wasn't as pretty as the wrapping
Your speech wasn't like poetry

You get the idea – each line asks the poet to argue with it, to prove it wrong. When I taught high school creative writing classes, my students particularly enjoyed this prompt. (Maybe the adolescent mind is wired this way.) Remember what it felt like to be in opposition to the world, and go from there. You might be surprised at what you find.

Haiku

At the Friends of the Los Gatos Library Bookstore, I found *Oasis in the Heart: Haiku with Exposition* by Toshimi Horiuchi (Shambhala Publications, 1995). In his introduction, Horiuchi writes "The true poet views the world with keen insight, sees much in little, and feels rapture even in what others might consider trivial or meaningless...a true haiku has something of an incantatory charm to store up spiritual and emotional energy in the human system."

45

Sometimes I go on haiku-writing binges. Here are four from the same day in September:

the zinnias
want to die
I keep watering

autumn fires
a woman calls for help
once she stuttered

digging
roots in damp soil
white hair

date on a penny
the year my father was born
worth more then

Haiku contain as much is energy as possible, squeezed into as few words as possible. They are powerful little packages, beautiful and provocative. To this day, Japanese haiku poets gather in walks called *ginko*, where they meditatively walk around fields and hills in order to create poetry.

Take a walk outside and write down what you see, hear, smell and touch. Create several haiku from a paragraph of reflection about nature. Share them with your friends.

Series

P oets don't usually write books with chapters, but they do, more and more it seems, write series of poems. A few examples: *Transformations* by Anne Sexton (Mariner Books, 2001) is a book of poems based on Grimm's Fairy Tales; *Here, Bullet* by Brian Turner (Alice James Books, 2005) is about Turner's experience as a soldier in Iraq and Afghanistan; and *Self-Portrait with Crayon* by Allison Benis White (Cleveland State University Poetry Center, 2009) deals with the author's life after her mother left, and then returned years later. There are many other examples: some writers take on the work of a visual artist, some explore their family histories, and others find inspiration in things as varied as the houses they've lived in, the pets they've owned, or the movies they've seen.

Find something that interests you. Does it lend itself to a series of linked poems? Where do you think it will lead? If you find yourself running out of ideas, do some research and go from there.

Here are a few suggestions:

Haunted places you've visited
Halloween costumes you've worn
Christmas trees: the good, the bad, and the ugly
Gifts from a person who always gets you what you want
Gifts from a person who never gets you what you want
Coins from different countries
Flights you've taken
Cities you love or hate – and why
Months of the year
Shoes
Books you read as a child
Tools
Electronic equipment – computers, cameras, phones, etc.

Brothers and Sisters

The theme of the 2011 issue of *Caesura*, the literary magazine of Poetry Center San Jose is "Brothers and Sisters." The call for poems about brothers and sisters included this: "Think blood brothers, brothers in arms, sisterhood is powerful, sisters of mercy. What do we mean when we call someone 'brother'?"

My poem, "Buck Moon," recalls two juxtaposed events: the birth of my youngest brother nine days prior to the first moon landing:

Erica Goss

Buck Moon

I didn't ask why my country was
moonstruck, deep in the month of July
when I was nine years old. I didn't
care about the stiff unflapping flag
and even less about steps, leaps or
mankind. I was not impressed with the
lunar module and its spider legs,
or the black sky, or a man's footprint.
I didn't know the US flag, fixed
upright in the bone-dry dust, was a
challenge to the world: *beat this*. I had
no idea who the Soviets
were. None of it mattered in that hot
July, for I received a brother,
knowledge that filled me with lovely pain
and made me dizzy, like when I caught
my first glimpse of a photo of Earth,
its blue surface mottled with storms and
continents, my head a whirlwind of
ragged energy, spinning, spinning,
breathless, euphoric, alive. Beat that.

Write a poem about your experience being a sister or a brother. If you are an only child, write about not having siblings. Imagine famous siblings, or siblings from fairy tales and mythology. How about Cain and Abel, or Hansel and Gretel? Did Jesus have a little sister? Use your imagination.

Try a Triolet

The triolet is a "fixed form from the middle ages, eight lines rhyming ABaAabaAB (the capital letters representing repeat lines or refrains" (from *The Poetry Dictionary*, John Drury, ed., Writers Digest Books, 2005). Robert Bridges, Dana Gioia, Sandra McPherson and Thomas Hardy have all written triolets.

I tried my hand at a triolet:

Erica Goss

Midnight Triolet

Midnight hones the appetite
blurring certain boundaries.
Corners round in candlelight;
midnight hones the appetite,
senses sharpen, eating life
greedy for huge quantities.
Midnight hones the appetite
blurring certain boundaries.

I like how the triolet, like the pantoum, uses repeated phrases, creating a sense of movement and a hypnotic rhythm to the poem. It simplifies things for the poet: come up with two really strong lines, and your job is half done.

Take a Walk

T ake a "look-see" walk with your digital camera. You can make this as long or short as you wish, but I usually need an hour to get some decent photos. This will not be a fitness enhancer, since the point of the walk is to notice the details around you. Take your time, and take lots of photos.

One summer day, I took a two-hour stroll down Summit Road in the hills above Los Gatos. I photographed these things:

Erica Goss

a cigarette butt next to a piece of orange peel
a llama
dozens of wooden fence-posts, mostly leaning west
a meadow of pale blonde grass
Mt. Loma Prieta
a baby redwood tree
a madrone tree with silver and red bark
a pine cone
mouse holes
snake holes
rattlesnake grass
road signs
the pavement
curves in the road
the sky

I added more information to the list after looking at the photos:

a cigarette butt next to a piece of orange peel (one bad for you, one good for you)
a llama (smelly but cute – watches me silently)
dozens of wooden fence-posts, mostly leaning west (San Andreas fault)

a meadow of pale blonde grass (what is that mysterious buzz-
ing? Burnt-coffee smell)

Mt. Loma Prieta (please stay put!)

a baby redwood tree (little green star – how can you get so
huge?)

a madrone tree with silver and red bark (like a peeling sun-
burn)

a pine cone (makes me think of Christmas in June)

mouse holes (there's a mouse living in the chicken coop)

snake holes (remember the king snake?)

rattlesnake grass (whisper/clink/shuffle)

road signs (new ones in bright yellow & black – yellowjacket
colors)

the pavement (all of the roads up here are falling apart – on
hot days you can smell the tar melting)

curves in the road (what's up there? Cal-Trans truck leaves
cloud of diesel)

the sky (horizon edged with fog over Santa Cruz)

Now the fun begins. I get to find the story in that random
list, use my imagination to glue these observations into a poem.
The camera shows me what it saw, not what I think I saw. It's
a very useful reference to keep going back to your pictures and
writing down more details as you remember them.

Erica Goss

Take a walk. Take your camera. Tell us what you found.

Something About the Birds

Birds: fascinating and mysterious, omens, messengers, enigmatic and ubiquitous—birds are everywhere and yet we understand so little of their lives. I regularly see and hear crows, jays, woodpeckers, juncos, finches, hummingbirds, gulls, doves, falcons, robins, and many others – but I have only the faintest idea of how they spend their days.

In 2012, Green Poet Press published *A Bird Black as the Sun, California Poets on Crows & Ravens* and includes poems by over 80 California poets, all about those strange black birds:

Erica Goss

Here is a sample from a poem by Joseph Stroud:

The night never wants to end, to give itself
over to light. So it traps itself in things: obsidian, crows.

List all of the birds you see in one day. Look for feathers.
Is there one bird you see more often? Why?

A final excerpt from "Lasswade, Midlothian: Dusk" by
Cecilia Woloch:

Crow, I cried, I need to talk to you.
The whole sky lurched…

Here is a sky that screams back at me
as I rush toward it, darkening.

I Scare Myself

What is your biggest fear? Be totally honest. Are you afraid of the dark? of losing your looks? of clowns, dogs, or old age? Capture all the details that startle you, terrify you, jolt you awake in the middle of the night. The more irrational, the better—as Mark Twain famously said, "I am an old man and have known a great many troubles, but most of them never happened."

Here are a few of mine: death, loss of loved ones, accidents on the highway, global warming, falling trees, having a bout of forgetfulness in the middle of a speech, perspiration, those gigantic beetles that show up on my screen door in the summer, running out of ideas, money, food…

Make a list of what you fear. Put a character in a dangerous situation and see what happens. Remember when you faced a fear and triumphed—or not.

How to Pirate a Treasure Chest

By Ellaraine Lockie

L ong before I became a professional poet/writer, I obsessively made notations of well-written sections or words that resonate in books I read, either underlining or listing word gems or phrases and their corresponding page numbers in the empty front pages of the books.

Erica Goss

One summer I cleaned out my library but couldn't stand to get rid of any books that had those notations, so I started a binder that I call my Treasure Chest where I listed every jeweled word that I recorded in the books.

The job was massive, as I'd never thrown away a book (not even the ones I'd marked *bad book*, for fear I'd forget and buy it again.) The binder was thick and gets thicker with nearly every book I read. Now, before beginning to read a book, I write its title and author's name on a blank, lined sheet of binder paper and place it in the back of the book. As I read, I list selected pearls of wisdom on the sheet with page numbers in case I want/need to quote or go back to the original source for context. If sections are longer than a short paragraph, I make a copy of the page, highlight the section and insert that in the binder.

Rewards consistently outsize the binder and the time/energy required by the process of creating it. Many times, as little as one word on the list has inspired an entire poem. Other times, a phrase or section will transport me to a related personal experience that I want to develop. Even when I'm not actively writing, I can get a literary thrill from just reading the list out loud. The Treasure Chest is also a great solution for writers' block and an investment for the future when old age may prohibit travel or physical interaction with the world in ways that previously served to inspire writing.

You don't need to have a life-long stack of books with notations to compile a similar Treasure Chest. You can begin with what you're presently reading. If you're an avid reader, as most poets/writers are, you'll soon have a healthy list of writing prompts. Of course, the language and images in any given book are only as good as that author's writing skills. I've found though that even a mediocre book, say a vacation fast-read, can still have sections that are Treasure-Chest worthy.

I use a real binder and actual papers because I internalize better when I apply pen to paper and when I then hold that same paper, as opposed to typing on a keyboard and reading from a computer screen. However, the process could be as successful in a computer file, especially if you read books electronically and can just scan the special sections into your designated file as you read the book.

Either way, you can have a wealth of writing tools and inspiration at your fingertips to pirate your own Treasure Chest at any time.

One Word

I found the word "languish" on the sidewalk a few weeks ago. As a poet, I'm always on the hunt for that special word, the one that will trigger some kind of response in poetry. I could hardly believe my luck in finding "languish." It made me remember the "one-word prompt," a writing exercise that I use often.

Find a word that moves you in some way. Now look it up in the dictionary and write down all of its meanings. "Languish" has these: 1. Be neglected or deprived; 2. Become less successful;

3. Pine. Aha! I see that "pine," both a verb and a noun, has possibilities. I start to wonder about the etymology of "pine," a word that signifies a tree and an emotional/physical state of suffering.

Look for a word that moves you in some way. Look up its various meanings, in both a dictionary and thesaurus. Look it up in a foreign language dictionary and see how it's defined in another language. Ponder its associations. Write.

Copy by Hand

Wat poet do you turn to, over and over, for inspiration? For me, it's the early work of Denise Levertov. Her simple, clear poems initiated me into the world of language as a young child. I can't claim that I understood the poems, or maybe only in a dim kind of way, but the line, rhythm, and images lodged in my brain and stayed there.

Take a poem by a poet whose work has influenced you and copy it, by hand (this is important!) on a piece of paper.

Erica Goss

Writing by hand slows you down and lets the words enter your consciousness. Now you have the poem, written in your handwriting, in front of you. Take another sheet of paper and start making notes about the poem: why does it move you? Do you think you could write something as good—or better? Why? Take a line from the poem and use it as the beginning of your poem. See where this takes you.

The Political is Personal

What makes a good political poem? It's difficult to convey historical events such as war, government upheavals, and their impact on our lives in poetry, but perhaps no more difficult than writing about other time-honored subjects such as nature, relationships, or art. With all topics, the key is to make the universal personal. Examining a story through the eyes of a witness, who might be you, a relative, or a historical character, is often a good place to start.

73

Erica Goss

To get a feel for how political poetry can move from the quotidian to the universal in one short sentence, here's the first line from "The End and the Beginning," a poem by the great Polish poet, Wislawa Szymborska: "After every war / someone has to clean up." The fifth stanza reads:

Photogenic it's not,
and takes years.
All the cameras have left
for another war.

The poet forces us to see not only "corpse-filled wagons," which we can easily imagine on our own, but the journalists who leave when the excitement is over.

A few years ago, I visited Berlin and stood where my father had stood as a young man when he was a GI. I imagined my father, twenty-three years old and homesick in a freezing winter, and all of the daring escapes that people had made when Germany was a divided country. I wrote the following poem as a result:

In Front of the Reichstag

When he stood here in 1956
my father decided to set his life to music.

American jazz, the language of home.
To learn forgiveness, listen to the blues.

Fifty years later
I step across the mended street

to read about the girl
who bent herself into a quarter note

and escaped to the West,
wedged into a stereo cabinet,

her body twisted
like the fossil Archaeopteryx.

She was so small, a gamine –
airy as the swan-bone flute

dug up in the Hohle Fels cave

Erica Goss

from which the oldest music comes.

Where else did the children hide –
crammed into cello cases, coiled into drums

as the little birds of Berlin
called out in tones of gold and mercy?

First printed in Lake Effect, *2011*

No matter how removed from our daily lives we think politics are, we experience their effects every day. Think about a soldier in Iraq or Afghanistan. What is his or her day like? What forces moved that person to join?

For some excellent examples of poetry that deals with war, politics and the consequences of both, I recommend *Here, Bullet* by Brian Turner; *The Country Between Us* by Carolyn Forché (Harper Perennial, 1982), and *Miracle Fair*, by Wislawa Szymborska (W. W. Norton, 2002).

Guidelines

By Connie Post

I used to write poems with a pre-determined idea in mind. I knew what I wanted to say and the metaphors that would most likely be used. Over the years, however I have changed the way I create poems. Now my poems often start with a simple line, or a few words, (even a news headline) that float around in my head for days, weeks or months. Or, there is an image, something I saw that spoke to me, that stayed with me and I think there is more to say. The writing is not usually immediate, but I hold the image, like a stone in my pocket, until the time is right. I usually write down the line or image in a "to be written" file and I access it often.

When I feel the time is right and the words or image have congealed, I start to begin. I never know when this will strike, but somehow I do know when *it's time*. This approach has led me down unexpected pathways. I let the line lead where it may. I let the image find its own story. I am often surprised by the direction of the poem. Even when I have a vague idea of what I intend to write, I like it best when the poem turns out in ways that surprise me. The line or image sometimes occurs as the title, but most often is embedded somewhere in the poem.

As an example of this, in 2007, the Mississippi River Bridge collapsed into the Mississippi. I watched the news stories and I was compelled. I imagined what it would be, to hear the collapse, how the descent must have felt. The news headline "Bridge Collapses into the Mississippi" was all I needed. I knew I had to write about it. I had no idea how the poem would turn out, or how it might end. But I started with the first line. About half way through the poem, I realized this poem was really about my disabled son. It has become one of my main poems to read, when talking about the devastation of having a son who will never speak. The journey of the poem, and its result occurs below:

"BRIDGE COLLAPSES INTO THE MISSISSIPPI"

– Star Tribune – August 1, 2007

When the concrete
finally surrendered
to the weight of buses
and shallow moons

when the open sigh
of the river
swallowed its own tongue

I imagine those cars
and what the hard edge
of water
must feel like

years will pass,

the screeching will
make unannounced visits
on nights

Erica Goss

when the river appears
to be sleeping

as I close my eyes
after the lamp goes off
I remember the day they told me
you would never speak

not one word

there would only be sounds

twenty years have passed since then

at times
I still find myself going back
to the elegiac banks of the same river

watching the water silently forgive itself
for not knowing
how to cease

Published in The Dirty Napkin *and winner of the* Dirty Napkin
Cover Prize *Spring 2009. Also published in* And When the Sun
Drops, *a chapbook by Finishing Line Press.*

God's Hobby

A little poem from *Verse Wisconsin's* April 2013 issue inspired this prompt:

Erica Goss

Making Butterflies

By K.S. Hardy

It must be
God's hobby,
Making butterflies,
Stooped over
His cluttered workbench,
A jeweler's glass
Wedged in his eye,
With tweezers in
Arthritic hands
Cautiously placing
The stained glass colors
In delicate wings,
His spit, his glue.

We imagine God as responsible for unforeseen catastrophes—earthquakes, floods and hurricanes are often called "acts of God"—but K.S. Hardy imagines the color and shape of a butterfly's wing as a gentler act of God.

God's Hobby

We all have leisure pursuits. Why not supreme beings?
If God had any spare time, wouldn't God spend it making
butterflies from Nature's infinite craft kit? On a rare day off,
would Athena attend sculpture class? Would Krishna practice
the flute? What do you think?

Poetry Bones

In the preface of *Writing Down the Bones*, Natalie Goldman writes "When I teach a class, I want the students to be 'writing down the bones,' the essential, awake speech of their minds."

Bones are pretty amazing things. The number of bones, and fossils of bones, that exists in just the state of Montana is truly astonishing. Bones tell us how people and animals lived and died, what they ate, and what diseases they may have had. If a bone breaks, that story lives on in the mended place. Bones frighten and fascinate us. Wherever we go, we leave bones behind; nothing tells the story of human history as accurately.

Metaphorically, bones stand for the structure of almost anything. A building has "good bones." People say, "I feel it in my bones." "Make no bones about it," we say when demanding total honesty, and "I have a bone to pick with you" when airing a disagreement.

A glance at my recent poems reveals that I use the word "bone" frequently: "paper, bones, glass" from "The Color She Wears;" "oil and bones" from "Bedroom Scene #5 (The Earth Rolls Over You) 2004, by Eric Fischl;" "alchemy, fish bones" from "Mother With Two Children, 1917, by Egon Schiele;" and "We're bones in October" from "Hunter's Moon."

Write down the bones. Find those essential things, the bones that hold us up, and explore their meanings. Go to a museum and look at some bones, or take a look at John Brosio's painting "Two Earthlings."

Strong First Lines

Certain poets have a way with first lines. Consider these from William Carlos Williams:

"Why do I write today?" (Apology)
"Sorrow is my own yard" (The Widow's Lament in Springtime)
"The rose is obsolete" (The Rose)
"It's the anarchy of poverty" (The Poor)

Else Lasker-Schüler begins her poem "Sabaoth" with the alluring and mysterious line "God, I love you in your gown of roses" ("Gott, ich liebe dich in deinem Rosenkleide").

And of course, the first line of Yeats's classic poem, "The Lake Isle of Innisfree" jumps off the page: "I will arise and go now, and go to Innisfree".

Each one of these first lines is an irresistible invitation to the rest of the poem, to the experience contained within it.

Study the first lines of great poems. Frost's "Mending Wall" starts with a negative: "Something there is that doesn't love a wall," a line that invites the reader to first puzzle over the slightly awkward phrasing, and then explore the rest of the poem, which climaxes with the couplet:

Before I built a wall I'd ask to know
What I was walling in or walling out.

Make a list of first lines that appeal to you. Practice writing strong leads to your poems. Imagine your reader flipping though a collection of poems, and pulling that reader in with the irresistible first line of your poem.

Strong Last Lines

Some poets are geniuses at wrapping up their poems. Some examples:

"illuminating a band of moving clouds." (Billy Collins, "Night Letter to the Reader")

"and I get more and more cockeyed with gratitude." (Billy Collins, "As if to Demonstrate an Eclipse")

Erica Goss

"Maybe he'd like a drink before we start." (Michael Heffernan, "Famous Last Words")
"Petals on a wet, black bough." (Ezra Pound, "In a Station of the Metro")
"I thought why not ride the rest of the way together?" (Linda Pastan, "Jump Cabling")
"true skin." (Nancy Eimers, "A Night Without Stars")

Poems with strong endings resist the impulse to trail off, something I've seen often in contemporary poetry. Weak endings can be appropriate to the poem they're ending, but generally they leave the reader unsatisfied. On the other hand, a strong ending line not only finishes the poem, but creates an opening for new ideas. Stephen Dunn's poem "Laws" starts with "A black cat wanders out into / a open field" and ends "The mice are constantly surprised." In between we get gems like "After humiliation, home is a hole / where no one speaks." The poem moves us steadily towards its deft conclusion, reinforcing its title and first lines.

Take a look at your own poems. Do the endings need a tune-up? Do the poems end on a weak note? Can you give your poems great ending lines?

A few more examples:

"Dearest," by Jean Valentine

"Glass" by Robert Francis

"We Real Cool" by Gwendolyn Brooks

"The Snow Man" by Wallace Stevens

The Sound of Poetry

On August 30, 2013, the world mourned the death of Seamus Heaney, one of our most accomplished and beloved poets. One of his many skills as a writer was his use of sound in poetry. Heaney's "The Rain Stick" is one of my favorite poems; in fact, I've read it in public so often that I've got it memorized. I particularly love the lines "You stand there like a pipe / Being played by water" and "You are like a rich man entering heaven / through the ear of a raindrop."

These lines from "The Rain Stick" describe the sounds a rain stick makes so well that I can hear them as I read:

Downpour, sluice-rush, spillage and backwash
Come flowing through…

A sprinkle of drops out of the freshened leaves,

Then subtle little wets off grass and daisies;
Then glitter-drizzle, almost-breaths of air.

I love the musicality of this poem, and how I instantly hear the "sprinkle of drops out of the freshened leaves," and how I get the joke that this dry thing, this cactus stalk, makes a sound exactly like rain. As soon as I read this poem, I wished I had written it. I've read it for audiences, for friends, for my father when he was far gone into dementia, for my husband, and to my children.

Describing sound is not an easy task in poetry. Beyond "loud" and "soft," we have a universe of noises, but selecting the ones that best fit can make or break a poem. A few more examples from Heaney: "Declensions sang on the air like a hosanna" ("Alphabets"); "The pump's whooping cough, the bucket's clatter" ("A Drink of Water"); "My serenades have been / The broken voice of a crow" ("Serenades").

Go out and listen today. Write down what you hear. Think of Ireland, with its haunting music and its poetry. What is the sound of loss? What did it sound like when you heard that Seamus Heaney had died?

Your Name

By Eileen Malone

Think about your name. Now begin writing, responding freely and spontaneously to the following:

How was it chosen for you? What do you feel towards it? What would you prefer it to be? What does it sound like when you say it? How have others mispronounced it and/ or misspelled it? What does it remind you and/or others of (famous or infamous people with the same name?) What are some nicknames derived from your name? When you were growing up, were you teased about your name? did anyone tell you who you were like with that name, or just the opposite of? Were you called by the same name written on your birth certificate. How is your name spoken when you are in trouble?

What color is your name? What animal? What plant? What weather? What number? What taste? What smell? What song goes with your name? What country?

Now take all your responses and jiggle, juggle them together into a poem that does not include the words "my name" anywhere. When finished, give it a title: one of the words or phrases therein.

Make a List

What happened when the French Surrealist poet, Andre Breton, wrote a poem in an ancient form known as the "blazon?" Lines like these:

My wife whose eyelashes are strokes in the handwriting of a child
Whose eyebrows are nests of swallows
My wife whose temples are the slate of greenhouse roofs
With steam on the windows
My wife whose shoulders are champagne

Erica Goss

Are fountains that curl from the heads of dolphins over the ice
My wife whose wrists are matches
Whose fingers are raffles holding the ace of hearts
Whose fingers are fresh cut hay
My wife with the armpits of martens and beech fruit
And Midsummer Night

From "Free Union" by Andre Breton

The blazon was originally intended to praise a woman's finer qualities, starting at the top and ending at the feet. It changed to include praising someone or something beloved, and when Breton used it in "Free Union," it became a wild collage of metaphors.

Praise someone, using the blazon.

:

Try a Different Language

If your titles are getting stale, try using words or phrases in another language. I've used this technique with the poems "Noche," "Encontrado," "Boden," and "Brot des Lebens" ("Night," "Found" (Spanish); "Soil," "Bread of Life" (German)). A title in another language can add a little intrigue and mystery to the poem. If the poem takes place in a foreign country, it adds depth to give it a title in that language. For example, "Noche" takes place in Mexico, and "Brot des Lebens" is about my German grandfather.

Erica Goss

Here are a few examples of poems written in English with
titles in other languages:

"Recuerdo" (Spanish: "Memory") by Edna St. Vincent Millay
"Puella Parvula" (Latin: "A Small Girl") by Wallace Stevens
"Guido, i'vorrei che tu e Lapo ed io (Italian: "Guido, I wish
that Lapo, you") by Robert Creeley (from Dante's "Sonnet to
Guido Cavalcanti")
"Ave Atque Vale" (Latin: "Hail and Farewell") by Nora May
French

Thirteen Little Poetry Projects

When giving poetry readings, I often hand out slips of paper, each containing a prompt from the list below. They are my favorites from "20 Poetry Projects," the creation of the late Jim Simmerman, a poet and professor from Northern Arizona University who died in 2006. I'm grateful for these little nudges in the direction of creativity, and refer to the list often. Mix them up; rearrange the list; choose three or four at random. You'll have fun, and you might get a poem out of it.

1. Begin your poem with a metaphor or a simile.
2. Say something specific but utterly preposterous.
3. Use at least one image for each of the five senses, either in succession or scattered randomly throughout the poem.
4. Use the proper name of a person and the proper name of a place.
5. Use a word—slang? that you've never used in a poem.
6. Use an example of false cause-and-effect logic.
7. Use a piece of "talk" you've actually heard.
8. Make the character in the poem do something he or she could not do in real life.
9. Refer to yourself by nickname and in the third person.
10. Write in the future tense, so that part of the poem seems to be prediction.
11. Modify a noun with an unlikely object.
12. Use a phrase from a language other than English.
13. Make a nonhuman say or do something human (personification).

Things That Get Me Writing

By Kelly Cressio-Moeller

1. Each time I go to a museum I head for the gift shop to
    buy a few postcards, but not always of work I especially
    like or have a connection with—it's an added challenge
    that gets my brain thinking in a different way. If nothing
    is coming from looking at what's in the actual painting/
    sculpture/photograph, then I create a narrative of what's

not in the frame, the story of what's happening just outside of it or what proceeds/follows it.

2. Watch a documentary film (Netflix has some gems streaming, PBS, NOVA, library rental) particularly of something you have no in-depth knowledge or something you would not normally watch—listen for one line or thought in that movie that captures you, begin there. It can go on to be the first line, an epigraph, or something that spurs you to research something further on the subject.

3. Listen to music—not as background, not while doing something else—sit in front of your music system and spend time fully listening to the music, preferably with headphones. This is also good to do if you are stuck in a poem or are blocked in some way.

4. Walking in nature will help loosen the cogs. Trees have helped me more than once.

5. Something else that works for me when I don't know where to go next in a poem is to insert a leap with an animal, plant, or mineral—at the very least this will get you thinking 'otherly' and can loosen the knots. Always works for me.

6. Subscribe to several 'word a day' sites—including Dictionary.com and foreign language sites like Transparent

Language—all free—and create a found poem from the words you gather over a week or several months.

Ode

According to Edmund Gosse (no relation), an ode is "enthusiastic and exalted lyrical verse, directed to a fixed purpose and dealing progressively with one dignified theme." Keats was an ode-writer par excellence, and one of my favorite poems of all time is "Ode on a Grecian Urn." How can one forget lines like "Thou foster child of silence and slow time," or "O, mysterious priest, / Lead'st thou that heifer lowing at the skies"? An ode is a poem of praise, somewhat like the blazon, but the subject can be almost anything.

Erica Goss

Kevin Young's "Ode to the Midwest" starts:

I want to be doused
in cheese

& fried.

  Go ahead. Try an ode. Elizabeth Alexander's "Praise Song for the Day," the poem she wrote for President Obama's first inauguration, is an ode.

Show, Don't Tell

I was recently asked how student writers of poetry could get better at cultivating images that "show" rather than "tell." I instantly thought of one of my favorite poets, Theodore Roethke, a poet who mastered that aesthetic. A good introduction to Roethke's work is found in the American Poets Project volume *Theodore Roethke, Selected Poems,* edited by Edward Hirsch.

Roethke, the son of German immigrants who grew up amidst the greenhouses his father tended near Saginaw,

111

Erica Goss

Michigan, wrote verse that, as Hirsch writes in his excellent introduction, "put language under intense pressure and developed a strange, highly kinetic, radically associative method." For a few examples of this technique in Roethke's poems, see the lines below (all are from The Lost Son and Other Poems):

"Sticks-in-a-drowse droop over sugary loam" ("Cuttings")
"Bulbs broke out of boxes hunting for chinks in the dark" ("Root Cellar")
"Thick and cushiony, like an old-fashioned doormat" ("Moss-Gathering")
"I have known the inexorable sadness of pencils" ("Dolor")
"Deep in the brain, far back" ("Night Crow")

"The Waking" uses the villanelle form to create what Hirsch describes as "a direct presentation of the unconscious making itself known." In the last stanza, Roethke delivers a mysterious conclusion:

This shaking keeps me steady. I should know.
What falls away is always. And is near.
I wake to sleep, and take my waking slow.
I learn by going where I have to go.

Notice the use of repetition in "The Waking," which contributes to the sense of the unconscious making itself known.

Read Roethke's poems. Try putting words under "intense pressure." What does that mean to you as a writer? Let your mind go where it might not have gone, but must in order to create fresh work. Let dreams linger – take your waking slow.

Parking Lots as Inspiration

Poets are inspired by nature: mountains, oceans, Yosemite, the stars. Those are endlessly fascinating, to be sure, but I read a lot of nature-inspired poetry that doesn't tell me anything new. I'll let you in on a secret: although I've written many nature-based poems, I find inspiration in parking lots. Yes, parking lots, ordinary stretches of asphalt that cover the ground, miles and miles of parking lots that surround buildings. I wonder what used to be there, before we needed a place to temporarily leave our cars. I look for the flaws and cracks that undermine every parking lot ever built.

Lanesboro, Minnesota, is a tiny town of about seven hundred. Recently, their visionary arts council decided to transform an ordinary parking lot into a Poetry Parking Lot. Instead of leaving the car in the lot while you go do something else, the lot itself became a destination. I call that brilliant.

Next time you're in a parking lot, take a look around. What do you see? What do you hear and smell? Each parking place is a little home for your car, gypsy that it is.

My poem "This is a Wild Place" began in a parking lot:

This is a Wild Place

On the last day of winter,
my car, filled
with chaff and spare parts,

fits neatly in its painted slot,
a motion box, stopped.
The little junk birds peck at foil,

and I am called away from my body
to forage for my life
out in the open.

When I was eleven
I climbed a huge pine
and had a vision

of flying into the thin
mountain air; my mother called
my name softly, standing on the red earth,

and her voice was a ladder
I climbed down.
I have seen the sky

in late winter, watched clouds
form the ribcage of a fantastic beast,
understanding that

the world is stitched together
from the loosest of tissues – even
concrete, webbed

with faint cracks

Erica Goss

leaves nooks
for the smallest seeds.

First printed in Café Review, *Spring 2010*

    You might not see the possibilities in parking lots, but I
challenge you to find some place that no else has claimed. Is it
the dumpster behind the fancy restaurant? A particular public
restroom? An alley or side street? Poems wait for you there.

Endings and Beginnings

If you keep a journal (and if you've been reading these prompts, you know I recommend recording your life in words and images) this is the time to go over it. I like to look at my photos from the year. Holidays, celebrations, birthdays, graduations—all signs of time passing.

Here's a prompt that can help you get started on writing a reflective poem, one that tells a story. Choose a line that can be used as both the beginning and the ending line. Now write down several memories, at least ten or fifteen lines worth (photos help with this). Play with the lines, moving them around until they make a story.

Here are some ideas for beginning and ending lines:

A news headline about a problem that never seems to be resolved
Children going back to school after summer vacation
A child going to school for the first time
Seasons passing
Holiday foods, served again, and again, and again (this could be the time to confess your dislike of cranberry sauce)
Clothing for specific weather (mittens, swimsuits, rain boots, shorts)
A recurring dream of a deceased loved one
Religious ceremonies

Heavy Roses

I like to collect books of postcards. Pomegranate Press puts out some nice ones, usually in sets of thirty cards, with reproductions from famous photographers such as Ansel Adams, Edward S. Curtis, Dorothea Lange, and one of my favorites, Edward Steichen. I'm drawn to the terse titles of Steichen's photographs: "Mullen," "Sunflower in a white vase," "Evening primroses, before 1928," "Sunday night on fortieth street, New York," "Heavy roses, France," "An apple, a boulder, a mountain."

(Pomegranate also has "New York Flashbacks," "Women of the West," "The Blue Planet: Photographs from NASA," and "Black Writers: Photographs by Jill Krementz," to name just a few.)

Buy a pack of postcards that are related in some way, either by the artist or by theme. Number them. Write a few words, a sentence, or a short paragraph on the back of each card, using the title of the art as the title of your poem. Here's an example:

#1: Florida Jungle (Edward Steichen, 1936)

I've never been to Florida
and this postcard isn't going there either
but it must be warmer than here

Address the card to yourself, affix a stamp, and drop it in the mail, in the order you wrote the cards. Do this every day until you've used up the cards.

In a few days, your cards will start to arrive in the daily mail. You'll be writing new postcard poems as old ones come back from the post office. Use this little event each day to enter into a dialog with the image and your words. Put the postcards in order and see what develops. There's a story in there, many stories in fact. Find them. Write them.

Stalked by Walt Whitman

I think I'm being stalked by Walt Whitman. For the last week, wherever I go I see a Whitman quote. I was in the San Jose Museum of Art, browsing their latest exhibition, when I read these lines from Whitman's poem "This Compost:"

"Something startles me where I thought I was safest,
I withdraw from the still woods I loved,
I will not go now on the pastures to walk,

I will not strip the clothes from my body to meet my lover the sea,
I will not touch my flesh to the earth as to other flesh to renew me."

I got home and opened *Ten Poems to Change Your Life* by Roger Housden, and read:

"These come to me days and nights and go from me again,
But they are not the Me myself."

Those lines are from the 1855 edition of *Song of Myself.*

That evening, I was browsing the web when I came across the Walt Whitman Mall in Huntington, New York, where there is an Apple Store.

I decided to pay attention to these messages from the poetry gods. What can we learn from Whitman to help us write better poems? How about this: stop worrying about writing better poems! Whitman was one of the most self-assured poets who ever wrote in the English language. His long lines, gently iambic, powerfully determined, are imbued with a very American optimism:

Stalked by Walt Whitman

And I know that the hand of God is the elderhand of my own,
And I know that the spirit of God is the eldest brother of my
own,
And that all the men ever born are also my brothers...and the
women my sisters and lovers,
And that a kelson of the creation is love.

Write long lavish lines about yourself. Call on the gods
and nature for assistance. You can start with one of Whitman's,
and then go from there. Loaf, and invite yourself.

Fifty Words

Many poetry prompt exercises ask you to make a list of a few words. However, I usually need a lot more words to really get going. I made a list of fifty words that appealed to me, for reasons unknown:

mystery cold sky blue red open read wind stone flight love amber snow dangerous free wonder secret move eye hand run morass kingdom nature bee caterpillar but-

**terfly ant wet bronze wait lips heart terror light birth
evening night winter fall encounter breathe lope chalk
little scream listen field soil cloud**

Every one of these words could be the title to a poem.
Take two or three and make new, more interesting titles. How
about "Wet Little Cloud" or "Listen, Bronze Caterpillar"? You
could alphabetize the list and make a fifty-line poem using each
word as the first or last word in every line. You could reverse
alphabetize the list and do the same.

The important thing is that you have a bunch of words
to play with, not just five or ten. There are at least 250,000
distinct words in the English language, according to the Oxford
Dictionary. Read them, understand them, use them.

Deep Images

Years ago, I was a student in a drawing class trying to draw a tree. My teacher came by and said, "What you've drawn is your idea of a tree. This is what you've been told, all your life, is a tree." My tree looked exactly like the trees I drew in elementary school. "You have to minutely observe something to stop seeing what you think it is, and see what it really is."

Erica Goss

Today we're going to look at something closely. Throw away your *idea* of what an object is, and try to understand what it *actually* is. The more carefully you look at something, the stranger it gets – that's because you're seeing details you don't usually pay attention to. Take any object. For example, I am looking at my desk lamp. If I describe its contour, I get this: "smooth, metal, screws, base, cord, bulb, switch, hinge, shade, arm, knob, arm, hinge, base…" and if I start to look at it more closely, I get "dusty, dead fly, scuff mark, silver, black, heavy, hot, too bright in that position, not bright enough in the other position, tilt, triangle thing the cord comes out of…" now I drill down again, and I get "casts shadow over my keyboard, makes the veins on my hands look like a topographical map, lights the tops of my books and the two-dollar bill I use as a bookmark, leaves my overstuffed files in the shadow." Hmm. There is a story in this ordinary desk accessory. Is my lamp a metaphor for something else? Isn't everything?

The experience of seeing this closely can simultaneously exhilarate and terrify. When I first saw a blown-up photo of a dust mite, it gave me the creeps for days, but I finally accepted the fact that the world is full of tiny, invisible living creatures.

Spend the day looking closely at things. Look at your children, your pets, your furniture. Look until you don't recognize them anymore. Write down what you really see.

Way Back

We're going way back for this writing inspiration. What is your earliest memory? Most of us don't remember much before our 5th birthday (except my brother, who has a remarkable memory of his early childhood). Yet, what happens to us before the age of five, when our brains are fresh and malleable, is of utmost importance. It's always seemed weird to me that we have no memory of our births. When do memories begin to form, and why?

Erica Goss

I asked members of my family for their earliest memories. Here's a pastiche of their responses:

"My cousins scaring me when I was a baby."
"Being the ring-bearer in my aunt's wedding when I was two."
"The giant crayons in front of my preschool when I was four."
"I was eight months old. I have a memory of a woman cooking in the backyard of our house in Mexico City."
"My father chasing a turkey behind the house."
"I was alone. I didn't know where my mother was, so I opened the kitchen window and started screaming. I think I was two?"
"Escaping from my bedroom to get the graham crackers from the kitchen. My sister cried because I wouldn't share, and my mom caught me. I was younger than two."
"I threw my underwear over the back fence. The neighbors brought it back at the end of a stick. I was about two."

My earliest memory is of my mother singing the German folk song, "Hänschen klein" ("Little Hans") to me. I was maybe two. That song is lodged forever in my brain.

Ask your friends and families to tell you their earliest memories. Make a list of things you remember from childhood. Let your mind wander back as far as it will go. Your poems will arrive, perhaps in a way that surprises you, from those bright flashes of childhood. Try to capture the wonder you felt as a child. When we read your poem, we'll experience it too.

Core Strengths

If you are familiar with the CrossFit exercise program, you know that it promotes a group of intense, varied workouts. These include the WOD (Workout of the Day), which is never the same set of movements two days in a row. The CrossFit faithful are convinced that the intensity and the variety of the exercises give them a superior workout.

What do a bunch of sweaty people yelling "arrrrgghhhh!" and throwing twenty-pound medicine balls around have to do with poetry? Well, plenty. If you ever embarked on an exercise program only to find that it became less and less effective, you understand the need to mix up your workout, whether it's physical or literary. Varying your writing routine can lead to new insights, a more confident tone, and can break you out of the creative doldrums.

Here are some suggestions to help you develop your core strength as a writer:

Change your writing routine. For example, you might be convinced you write better in the wee hours of the morning, or in the afternoon, or at midnight. Try writing at the time of day when you normally feel less effective.

Practice writing in short, timed bursts. Set a time limit—say five minutes—and write. Then decrease the time by a minute until you're down to one minute. Then decrease it to thirty seconds. Learning to write this way can be very helpful when you get a sudden inspiration but you're not at your desk.

Change your location. I don't mean swap your nice comfy desk for the local café—that's too easy. Remember, we're using

CrossFit for a model here! Take your notebook to a place you have never written before: the edge of the ocean, an animal shelter, the freeway overpass, a construction site, a karate studio, an appliance store, a gas station, a preschool, a pharmacy. Practice those short, timed bursts. Don't worry if you attract attention.

Vary your reading diet. Always stick to free verse of a certain period? Try some of the New Formalists. Tend to read mostly people of the same gender and ethnic group as yourself? Well, there's really no excuse for that—but sometimes it takes an effort to seek out what's different. Read more challenging work, and don't give up right away.

Write a bunch of poems with titles like "Squat," "Deadlift," "Dips," "Rope Climb," "Pull-ups," and "Holds." Make them muscular. Make them sweat. Then do it again.

Work It Out

By Evelyn A. So

Write about a physical activity. Here are a few possibilities to get you started: swimming, running, dancing, walking, hiking, driving a car, taking a bus or train. Try to include sensory details for the senses of sight, sound, touch, smell, and taste to help convey a vivid impression of this experience. You may also wish to consider whether you would like to convey the activity that you have chosen to write about positively, negatively, ambivalently, or indifferently.

Fruitcakes

Food is one of my favorite topics for poetry. The Spring 2009 issue of Caesura, Poetry Center San Jose's literary journal, was devoted to food. I was the co-editor, and we had fantastic poetry from Diane Lockward, Jane Blue, Bill Keener, Robbi Nester, Paul Hostovsky and many others.

As I wrote in the introduction, "Food is survival, and so much more: memory, pleasure, tradition and culture." A few titles from the issue: "Ars Poetica as Porridge Breakfast in Paris"

Erica Goss

(Greta Aart), "Not Exactly Millefiori" (Lianne Spidel), "Corner Restaurant, Butter Pats Shaped Like Ducks" (Susana Case).

When writing about food, we can involve all of the senses: taste, appearance, aroma, texture, and even sound, as in the crunch of carrots rattling in the ear. Treasured recipes speak of family connection and love.

I wrote this poem about the much-maligned fruitcake.

About Fruitcakes

Many people feel that these cakes improve greatly with age,
though not everyone agrees.
— Joy of Cooking, "About Fruitcakes"

A cake that takes a month to set
brooding in its rum-soaked wrap;
a cake robust with strange sweet fruit
waits for us on Christmas Day.

No one really likes it
sticky with its offbeat parts,
raisins, kumquats, pineapple,
citron, cherries, lemon peel

fermented with alcohol
and proudly served by the elderly.
Some have based their comedy
on insults aimed at fruitcake

but long before the jokes and jabs
our grandmas chopped and snipped and sliced
saving bits of this and that,
insurance against leaner days.

Nights grow darker, cold and wet
as the year comes to its end.
Appreciate the fruited cake –
some things do improve with age.

This poem is really about my Oma, my dad's mother, whose
fruitcake was a marvelous concoction of nuts and candied
fruits, held together with butter, eggs and a generous soaking
of rum. As a child, one slice left me a little tipsy as the cake
settled into the pit of my stomach.

What food reminds you of a beloved grandparent, or a country
of origin, or a childhood event? What food do you associate
with a holiday? What food do you secretly crave, or openly

Erica Goss

detest? Go through the grocery store and make a found poem from food labels. Try this at different stores – an upscale, organic market, a Walmart, a convenience store. Find the story, and write it down.

Food I'm From

By Evelyn A. So

Write a poem about food, using a refrain that begins with the phrase "I am from…" or "I'm from…" and using the list poem form to list different food groups. This prompt has been very popular in my teaching experience with fifth grade students or younger as well as with high school students and adults. The prompt can easily be adapted into a fun icebreaker so those responding to it also learn more about each other in the process.

Fairy Tales

F airy tales are not just for children. The stories the brothers Grimm collected, for example, are frequently dark and disturbing, even in the sanitized versions we've adopted.

In 2005, I visited the Märchenwald (Fairy tale forest) in Altenberg, Germany. What a gently peculiar place it was, in a mysterious green park of tall trees hung with moss. Here you can view mechanical puppets of Snow White and the Seven Dwarves in a tiny cabin, complete with seven miniature beds, or push a button and watch Rapunzul's golden hair erupt from a stone tower. Everything is child-sized, including a special section of the restaurant just outside the park. It's rumored that Walt Disney visited this Märchenwald, looking for ideas for Disneyland.

Something I noticed about Märchenwald was that the frightening elements of the Grimm fairy tales—giant crows, wolves, and evil queens—were not removed from the little houses and displays. Good and evil stood side-by-side. The balance between light and dark struck me, unlike the artificial perfection of Disneyland.

The best poems are a balance between light and dark. They don't dwell in either, but include the full range of human experience. Snow White must eat the poisoned apple, and the wolf will devour Red Riding Hood. These archetypes can be fertile ground for poems.

One of my favorite fairy tales as a child was "The White Bear," in which a young girl, sold by her parents to an enchanted prince, loses him and then rescues him from an evil fairy. My poem, "The White Bear," is based on that story:

The White Bear

*A man came and lay down beside her, and behold it was the White
Bear, who cast off the form of a beast during the night.*
— *The Blue Fairy Book*

Too young for regrets or suspicion
I climbed his thick body

watched one paw lap over the other
claws tilted inward as I held on
and we swayed down the road.

Back home mama and the children
stared at the dirt floor. Papa counted
pieces of gold.

I walked away from my childhood,
little breasts a surprise on my chest.

What would love be like?
Mama and papa: rustling, a groan.
Seven children among the dented pots.

Each night I put out the light. Only then

Erica Goss

did he come to me, pull back the furs
and slide his hands up my arms,

the hands of a prince:
calloused from the sword
and the grip of his fingertips.

Our bed burned those Nordic nights.
Days were empty and twilit. Still a child

I listened for his breathing, tilted the candle
over his noble head. Now
I go begging from door to door

looking for him in cities, in men's faces
our pale baby strapped to my back
her hair like the snow

that piled up outside the long hall
corners dwindled
and dark with enchantment.

First published in The Bohemian Journal, *Fall 2012*

Study a favorite fairy tale. List its main characters, and then chose one to tell the story. Try Hansel's father, Snow White's stepmother, or the man who brought the straw for Rumpelstiltskin to spin into gold.

Assemblage for Poetry

Assemblage is an art form that consists of repurposing found objects into 3D collages. It's a useful tool for the writer, as well, especially if that writer keeps a fairly consistent journal.

I recently wrote a poem made largely of lines from my journal that I collected over a period of weeks, and then sat down to see if they connected.

157

October 7, 2013: "The joyful bounce of an insect as if air was a giant fluffy bed meant for playing on."

October 8: "I love when a book comes with a map or a family tree."

October 9: "I love that my 'lite' breakfast comes with two slices of bacon."

October 20: "I love it when a man well past youth speeds past me on his bike, arms outstretched, head bare, and the smile of the boy he used to be glowing on his face like the gap-toothed grin from a jack-o-lantern."

These little scenes struck me with their humor or irony, but I had to figure out why I'd noted them, and the story that would link them. The resulting poem, titled "The Weight of So Much Compassion," ended up being a kind of ramble through the month of October, with flashbacks and fast forwards, trips to the past and anxieties about the future, and arranged itself in long lines that flowed across the page.

I like this poem for the following reasons: it surprised me to write it, but it's authentically my voice; I don't usually write long lines, but I found a rhythm and sound pattern that pleased me and helped keep the sentences strong; and it really feels like an assemblage, even though I wrote the lines myself, so it's not properly a "found" poem.

Start with an observation, something comical or sad that strikes you. Write one such insight down every day for a couple of weeks. Find the story, and let the poem dictate its form. Allow yourself to ramble, to add lots of adjectives, and then cut until the poem emerges, beautiful and surprising.

Using the Tip of a Medium Ball-point & Black Ink

By Pushpa MacFarlane

Than this might not sound so sophisticated, but mostly, this is enough for me to get writing. Of course, I always carry my notebook, but at a pinch, any paper will do—even a scrap of toilet paper has served more than its purpose.

Reading and free writing works well for me every time. Sometimes, I might pick a poet I like. Other times, I might want to sample a poet I've never heard of, or never read. I've also enjoyed reading poems from an anthology, so I can be surprised by the variety of inspiration it presents.

One thing I've tried to practice is noting down what I like about a poem I've just read, and particularly, how the poem inspires me. In doing so, I am able to learn some detail I might have otherwise overlooked or forgotten, if I didn't jot it down. I also note how the poet handled descriptions, how the poet worded a phrase, or how a narrative was handled, and of course, any new vocabulary. Doing this gives me a chance to try new techniques to see if they work for me.

Most times, in the middle of reading, I might be reminded about something in context, from my own life or something similar I've experienced, and I start writing, letting the thoughts flow onto the page without pausing. My mind is awake, my observation at its peak, my sense of humor upright, ready to take off.

You might wonder why I'm specific about using black ink. I see the blue ink as an impediment that makes me stop and tread more carefully. If I start reading what I've written, the nagging editing perks up, stalling my thoughts. The black ink just runs along like my thoughts, moving on the page, sometimes running rampant like a planchette on a Ouija board—never bored, the words tumbling down and scooting across the page. It's almost exhilarating.

I rarely read what I've written right away. I let it marinate there in my notebook. Most times, I already have a title. In fact, I jot down creative titles of poems I'd like to write, before I've written a word. For me, the title inspires the poem and I'm stimulated to write it. Almost like picking a name for an unborn child. That's how naturally titles come to me.

You'll probably see me carrying my tote bag around, with a couple of books, my medium tipped black ink pen and notebook, so I have something to read either on the light rail, or at a coffee place, if I'm waiting somewhere, or even if I'm at a bookshop or the library, or watching TV. You never know when you might be inspired by something you come across.

I find myself continuously thinking, observing, and mentally making notes. There's a whole world outside of myself, and somewhere, there is always a story brewing.

Suggested Reading

Addonizio, Kim and Laux, Dorianne. *The Poet's Companion*, W. W. Norton, 1997.

Boisseau, Michelle and Wallace, Robert. *Writing Poems*, Harper Collins, 1996.

Hugo, Richard. *The Triggering Town, Lectures and Essays on Poetry and Writing*, W. W. Norton, 2010 (reissue).

Levertov, Denise. *New & Selected Essays*. New Directions, 1992.

Lockward, Diane. *The Crafty Poet*, Wind Publications, 2013.

Oliver, Mary. *A Poetry Handbook*. Mariner Books, 1994.

Padgett, Ron. *The Teachers & Writers Handbook of Poetic Forms*. Teachers & Writers Collaborative, 1987.

Rukeyser, Muriel. *The Life of Poetry*. Paris Press, 1996 (first published in 1949).

Wiggerman, Scott and Meischen, David. *Wingbeats: Exercises and Practice in Poetry*. Dos Gatos Press, 2011.

Wooldridge, Susan G. *Foolsgold: Making Something from Nothing and Freeing Your Creative Process*. Harmony, 2007.

Wooldridge, Susan G. *Poemcrazy: Freeing Your Life with Words*. Broadway Books, 1997.

Notes & Hyperlinks

"Delusions of an Erasure Poet: the Shadow text," page 29, by Dave Bonta: http://www.vianegativa.us/category/poems/pepys-diary-erasure-project/.

"Short on Time? Try a Zip Poem," page 35, by Jennifer Swanton Brown: link to Michael Dylan Welch's blog, "Graceguts:" https://sites.google.com/site/graceguts/

Page 36, "Zips" by John Carley: http://www.poetrymagazines.org.uk/magazine/record.asp?id=4653

Page 37, World Haiku archives:
http://whrarchives.wordpress.com/2011/09/13/editors-choice-short-verse-zip-haiku/

"Variations on a Theme," page 41: link to Sir Edward Elgar's Enigma Variations, Royal Philharmonic Orchestra: http://youtu.be/La727Hbly8Q.

"Poetry Bones," page 86: link to the artist website of John Brosio: http://www.johnbrosio.com/figurescapes_one.html.

Credits

Joie Cook, "There Are Nights In San Francisco." Copyright © 2013 by Joie Cook. Reprinted with permission of David Picariello.

CrossFit is a registered trademark of CrossFit, Inc.

Mark deCarteret, "fable" from *Bigger Than They Appear: Anthology of Very Short Poems* (Kentucky: Accents Publishing, 2011). Copyright © 2011 by Mark deCarteret. Reprinted with permission of the author.

K.S. Hardy, "Making Butterflies" from Verse Wisconsin, April 2013. Copyright © 2013 by K.S. Hardy. Reprinted with permission of the author.

Paul Hostovsky, "Nose" from *Bigger Than They Appear: Anthology of Very Short Poems* (Kentucky: Accents Publishing, 2011). Copyright © 2011 by Paul Hostovsky. Reprinted with permission of the author.

Peggy Landsman, "Silhouette" from *Bigger Than They Appear: Anthology of Very Short Poems* (Kentucky: Accents Publishing, 2011). Copyright © 2011 by Peggy Landsman. Reprinted with permission of the author.

Mary Lou Taylor, "When I First Awoke" from *The Fringes of Hollywood* Copyright © 2002 by Mary Lou Taylor. Reprinted with permission of the author.

Acknowledgments

I would like to thank Jan McCutcheon and Steve "Spike" Wong of PushPen Press for believing in this book and for their help and encouragement. Thanks to the poets whose work appears on these pages for the gift of their work. Finally, my deepest gratitude and love goes to my husband, Don, without whose support this book would not be possible.

Erica Goss is the Poet Laureate of Los Gatos, CA, and the host of **Word to Word, a show about poetry**. She is the author of *Wild Place* (Finishing Line Press, 2012). Her poems, reviews and articles appear widely, both on-line and in print. She won the 2011 Many Mountains Moving Poetry Contest and was nominated for the Pushcart Prize in 2010 and 2013. Please visit her at: www.ericagoss.com.

9459030R10117

Made in the USA
San Bernardino, CA
18 March 2014